SCENES FROM LIFE O

KATHRYN SIMMONDS

Scenes from Life on Earth

SALT

CROMER

PUBLISHED BY SALT PUBLISHING 2022

2 4 6 8 10 9 7 5 3 1

First published in Great Britain in 2022 by
Salt Publishing Ltd
12 Norwich Road, Cromer, Norfolk NR27 0AX United Kingdom

www.saltpublishing.com

Salt Publishing Limited Reg. No. 5293401

A CIP catalogue record for this book is available from the British Library

ISBN 978 1 78463 277 9 (Paperback edition)

Typeset in Sabon by Salt Publishing

Printed and bound in Great Britain by Clays Ltd, Elcograf S.p.A

In memory of my mother

Contents

Rhododendron

Anything now brings her to mind.   In the wrong
dullness of May it is the rhododendron bush
manufacturing   its impossible flowers,
great shaggy petals of cerise   that 80s shade
which once was everywhere.

Evening's fetch & carry done,
my girls are settling to sleep,   their small histories
boggle and blur   beneath a first light layer of dream.

The garden spreads with shadow greens and greys
but still the rhododendron flares,

and there's my mother, patient at her mothering,
stationed outside a cubicle in Tammy Girl
re-hanging blouses I've cast off,
their crumpled hot-pink petals scattering the ground.

Dandelions

They pitch up overnight, a festival
on every verge, settle
        where their own seed blows,

the living
tangled with the dead,

raggy spats of yellow
making merry on their hollow stems

beside the elegantly spent,
        heads like tiny
empty pincushions.

Why dandelion?
        Why this roaring regal name?

                I swish for answers,
find an aberration, lion's tooth –
dent de lion –
        given for the flower's jagged leaf,

and folk names too, *milk witch*,
monk's head, faceclock,
        also *piss-a-bed*.

Though beloved by bees
and herbalists,
we labour to be rid of them,

tough as worries
they'll not yield –

for each loose beauty
        with a trailing root

        a dozen struggles
ending with a snap –
        one milky eye
        stares back;

our curses fall
            like so much rain.

And yet, who couldn't love their tricks?
        The way they'll force
        their heads
                through paving cracks,

the way the flowers shrink to pods
preparing to explode

into a wobble globe,
        transfigured,
        puffed up white with death,

waiting to be scattered by the wind
        or grabbed for,
held to light
                so clouds race through,
        and sun alerts
each seed spore to itself,

blown with a child's breath,
blown like luck

to ride on air,
more life!
More life!

Doll's House

The doll's house wants for windows
and a proper paint job.
Half the floors are carpeted
and half bare board.
It's liveable despite the lack of toilets.
The roof lifts up. The walls swing out:

there's Daddy fully clothed and showering,
slumped against the cubicle, his son
face down on the floor outside.
There's big sister at her computer,
orange wool hair flying straight up to the sky.
Her little sister's at the kitchen table,
feet shod in wooden shoes,
never finishing a meal.
The empty fridge is on its side in the attic.
The pink sheet grass is wrinkled all around.
And Mummy lies on her hard bed
in the middle of the afternoon,
dreaming with her eyes open.

Tomato Plant Survival Song

In a terracotta pot
ambition staked to a broken cane, and nameless (for the lolly stick
has blown away)
I pull at hope
without a tap root.

My character is lack: lack of vigour, lack of flower, lack
of what it is to be to-ma-to.
Not tomato,
nor suggestion of tomato.

The Moneymakers and Gardener's Delight
continue ravishing, predictably,

but I'll have no self-pity,
no suspicions of this third-rate   third-use
potting compost,

light and leggy as I am   yellow at the lower leaves
I'll not lament disease:

I need my sugar fuels to live.
From veiny hour to hour
I live.

Nothing escapes me
          woodlice roll their silver stomachs,
bees sip the sweet pea's
               intimate interior.

The fearful caterpillar undulates and crawls. It shall become.
Unless that blackbird has it
(or the starling
trembling the washing line).

At night when foxes screech inside their filthy quilts
I breathe their stinking musk –

shit-perfume
fragrance these splotched leaves. Season my dream.

III

Slugs!

Their terrible soft mouths.

New shoots in tatters,
done for.
Why doesn't she bring salt?

Why only frowns and secateurs?

Aphids! Aphids! Look!
Their icky feet, their hairs
upon my hairs.

She lifts my blighted leaves
notices four flowers
        dangling abortively and
pinches them away.   No tom-a-to.
Will she wait?

I remember that nasturtium, how it bolted, how it shrank, how she finall
      up-ended it
broke its feeble systems in her hand.

I am alone and thirsty.
                Let midsummer showers come.

IV

It persists.

(Fear of death has made it whimsical,
and on occasion now it speaks about itself
in third person,
which allows for rest, and oh it wants to rest).

There is no rest.

Grow, it whispers to its planted brain.

V

        Sun!
        Sweet rain!

In fresh light: blackbird song.
               From open windows
a guitar
effortful at first
        before a run of notes.

VI

What alchemy?

See   little tranche
of light fittings
hidden   under leaf?

Switch on! Switch on!

Sky cloudy white   take up this yellow prayer.

VII

All day, all night
                petals whisper *we'll become*

a bulb of green, oh small
machine of longing,

first dream of fruit, hung
like modest earrings

swelling green   becoming
pale orange   pale red   ripe scarlet

gladness edible.

Sing your songs for I am entering myself
I have become tomato

O tomato   I am the thing I am!

Dragonfly

This electric stem
of aqua black
appears from air,
surfs a grass blade
flightless for a while, eyes
precarious as sugar bowls
on a table edge,
and looks at what?
At what is green and dense
and tangles here,
doesn't fear but lets
itself be looked at.

So I turn from bulrushes,
their slumping slow platoons,
their dying flower heads,
and kneel in this royal
mess of grass, where dogs
have doubtless pissed, happy
to pay witness as the insect
witnesses itself,
a dropped jewel
or a frail god
glowing at the river's
muddy bank.

Wednesday Morning

In the supermarket café
I see my mother's freckled hands,
her face opening
and closing to the world.
The *blip* of tills goes on, the coffee machine.
I dress her in a scarf she liked, one
from the multitude massed in her drawer,
pale blue with indigo swirls,
and think of that Modigliani print
of a long-necked woman,
gifted by her colleague,
bought because he said there was
'a certain lanky elegance' they shared.
She laughed, delighted to be teased,
hung the picture on the stairs,
and her laugh tumbles loose,
a bolt of silk unravelling.
At the next table a small girl settles
with her grandmother, white sprig
of pony tail, fresh feet buckled into sandals.
I strain to touch the blue scarf
while the grandmother halves
a cup-cake, and the mother arrives with coffee.
Their shared stance, the leaning way
they sit. The grandmother spoons cake
into the child's mouth, and the mother talks,
an eye on the spoon, about a bird feeder
she'd like to buy. She describes
this bird feeder at length
and her mother nods, still spooning cake,
asking questions here and there against the *blip*
of groceries being scanned,
the coffee machine doing its work,
and as they chat the women instinctively

take turns to lay a hand on the little girl
or say a word to make her smile.
It is such an ordinary Wednesday.
At an outside table an old man in a short-sleeved shirt
reads his newspaper with a magnifying glass.
His arms are mottled, stained like wood.
They say summer's finally arrived.

Solstice

Ten o'clock
and the trees are black
against a still-blue sky.

Outside my window
one bird
moves about its home

crashing in the branches
repeating itself
endlessly,

a solitary maniac.
I'm tired out
but on it goes, my heart

as bird, there in that tree
thrashing, fretting
saying only this:

WhatisWhatisWhatis?

Aged Nearly Three

days have no names
and all days in the past are yesterday.
Yesterday, Mischa come to visit us.
Yesterday, Grandma poorly.
She runs her nakedness about the house,
squeals to be caught,
a greased piglet at the fair.
She detests that boring place
where she must sit still like a penitent,
prefers sometimes a puddle on the floor.
She will withhold a kiss
commanding you to cry until you mock-sob
to yourself, only then will she console
with exaggerated grace.
She will roar and make
the face of terror followed by delight.
Standing slumped over the sofa
lets you know all is not well:
she's bored, there will be consequences.
Her tin box is the portable home for all
the plastic bits of broccoli and fairy beings,
teacups ('cupatea?'), Lego people, insects,
glittered ladybirds. She will talk to them
and let them live their lives
expansively, until they're left for dead
and she's away,
off to find her sister's things
attainable 'til half past three.
She plays *This Little Piggy* with my toes
and feels her hand about the rough whorls of my heels.
She finds the photograph of me at her age, dancing.
'Who's that?' I ask.
'Me!' She says.
'No, it's me.'
She laughs, it is the best joke in the world.

Inside the Whale

She will have peril:
Daniel locked in with the lions,
or Goliath felled like a tree.

Tonight we're fleeing God with Jonah,
clambering aboard a ship bound for Tarshish
before that plunge into a freezing sea,
and though we've read this chunk of ancient
storytelling many times, tonight it's true,

truer than anything I know to be,
for who hasn't known the inside
of a whale's belly,
how it feels to crouch there
in a breathing cave

not seeing any world outside,
only rocking over waters,
eyes closed, longing for deliverance.

Premier Inn

You, who have been sought in all the lonely places,
     (should my mouth be berries and ash)
will you come to this locked room? Will you come
     in dimmed-down dark, a purple sash
across the bed? (Should I find myself a cell, a heath instead).

     The en-suite is electric, white as paradise,
its articles of faith un-bagged, arranged: toothbrush,
     moisturiser, shower gel, and just in case
a box of paracetamol – everything designed to keep us fresh,
     to keep us safe & well.

The flat-screen sleeps, the Wi-Fi is at rest, though it
     can never be at peace. Be near me now. I feel
an emptying out and hear a stifled spill from pub to street
     as farewells scatter on the night. A car door slams.

I'm four flights up and sealed in.
Will you come? My arms
     are open and I wait, poised on the brutal
               creases of this sheet.

Leaf Song

Better to be leaf.
Better to belong
to tree, to be
a twinkling
rotting bit of it than
walk about all day
tormented by a brain.
Better to be leaf,
free from all that inside
stuff which drowns
the breezes, bronze
and buffeting,
better to be leaf,
decisionless, alert
and in community,
dependent on the tree
entirely – old majesty.
Better to be leaf,
yellow with September's
creep then edging
orange. Better that
than living forty feet
below and moving on
two cranky legs, dead
fast, dead slow, talking
to your own self
all day long, alive
and living with a heart
that whispers with
the facts and doesn't
beat about the bushy
truth. Better that,
better to belong
to tree, to be a twinkling

rotting bit of it, light
veined and lipless
in the chill bright air.

Spencer in the Wilderness

'. . . I loved it all because it was God and me all the time.' – STANLEY SPENCER

When life had gone awry and there was nowhere
he could lay his head, he found a room
to rent and shut himself away
to paint Christ in the wilderness,
a fleshy, hungering saviour robed in white.

The plan was forty paintings for the forty days
and nights of Lent, small canvas squares intended
for the Church House, that building which would never be,
although he carried every wall inside his head,
furnished every cove with what he loved,
not his *Ascot fashions*, nor his *sweet-pea colours*,
but dirt and angles, the commingling of God and mud.

Swiss Cottage shakes off rain, a smattering of blossom
falls from life. Another Christ takes shape,
this one intent upon the insect in his palm,
a scorpion poised to strike, to pain.
Its moment will not come, only this everlasting meeting point.

After solitude the work will carry on,
steel landscapes, resurrection scenes –
bodies heaving up through paving flags
while linen flaps on washing lines and children
pause a game to stare.

For now, all life is in this room. His needs are few.
Consider the lilies of the field: he does,
recalls his daughter Shirin
as an infant, a glorious wondering child
who Christ becomes, crawling on all fours
to contemplate the daisy-scattered grass.

Spiders

On the thread of
this attempted prayer
a hair braced attentively

I lower down,
the slightest give
a catch only the heart

can feel, and think
of spiders,
their secret spinnerets,

how these September days
when opening
the greenhouse door

I've walked face first
into a web
no one could know

was there except
the crumpled maker.
I've spun nothing

and hang in nothing,
my thread invisible unless
glossed by light,

lowering down into air,
or what is not air
but the belief of it.

In April

Nothing better than to sit beneath this cherry tree with
    nothing needing to be done, to read

while bees are being bees, and all the birds murmur
    of anaphora – are they sick of

formalism and the avant-garde? If only
    there were music, never mind its provenance,

then what a garden we'd be in. Bits of blossom drift
    towards the rented grass. Meanwhile

the book grows sad, each paragraph creeps deeper
    into shade. Lay it down then, make a study

of the rhododendron bush, those scruffy
    flowering chives, and there that vivid orange

something with its pointy envelopes, offering
    an origami show. A breeze arrives, the birds grow

raucous in warm sun – Nature dandles me as if I were
    her one beloved child – and here's more blossom

lovingly detached, shedding its peeled fingertips
    across my shoulders, blessing my aging toes,

it gathers in my hat without insisting on its own
    significance, and when I rise, it lets me go.

Ambition

Oh you, old gods,
what a spectacle we are to you,
always wanting.

At night I read a fairy story
of a fisherman who catches and releases
an enchanted fish. His wife

forces him (the wife, always)
to ask the fish for more, for more,
and so they swap the hovel for a cottage,

the cottage for a castle, the castle for
an emperor's palace. Sure enough
they find themselves again in rags.

What little worlds revolve inside
our little worlds? Who are those people
we think we want to be?

The Death of Want

If wanting was dead, what would we
replace it with?

≫

The opposite of fear, I read,
is not courage but trust.
Who could ever trust herself
                    not to want?

≫

The jars of want toppled from the highest shelf
and smashed into astonishing fragments on the supermarket floor.

Don't pick them up! Yelled staff from another aisle.
You'll cut yourself!

≫

Inside closed rooms
the wants appear.
Some fly like ghastly bloodsucking bats,
others struggle to open their wings
and fall from table edges.

Where are the gorgeous butterflies?

≫

All the strongest characters have clear wants.
But the author knows that want
is not the same as need.
Don't she remembers, poised above the keypad
Give them what they want.

℗

In some places you can't do what you want.
You have to be taught to do what someone else wants
and pretend the want is your own.

But relinquishing your want
is like pretending someone else's baby
belongs to you:
even with your eyes shut
you know the smell is wrong.

℗

He wanted her unconscious to stop being so loud.
Can't you hear it? he asked.
Can't you do something about it?
It's keeping me awake at night.

℗

Ignatius counselled attentiveness,
Know what the heart wants,
your deepest desire will lead to God.

I wanted to want what God wanted.
I didn't know what that was.

&

Wonton soup, she said.

I saw wants floating
over chicken broth.

&

When he was young,
he wanted to be older.
When he was older
he wanted to be younger.
Now he is dead
and doesn't want for anything.

&

In English, there is no rhyme for want.
Won't perhaps
that might be nearest.
But wait –

My want was baptized in the *font.*

&

I want never gets.

Sometimes.
I want *sometimes* gets.

　　　　　　　　　⁊℥

If I found want and scooped it up, how would it look?
Its knees tucked in, little tender knees, crunched
like a dog begging.
Or a woman in some painful yoga pose.

　　　　　　　　　⁊℥

It's just a word, like warring and waning.
Like will and won't.
Want. Repeat it.
Make it meaningless.

　　　　　　　　　⁊℥

When the King wanted cherries
the Queen wanted braised pheasant and no sauce.
When the King shouted at the Queen
the Queen looked at him.
What a fool!
How could I ever have wanted this?

　　　　　　　　　⁊℥

Some wants we hardly recognise.

Others stay young forever.

⁊ᴓ

I went wanting,
a-wanting I went.
They made me a folk song for my wanting.
Now I sing it, evenings, afternoons, and always without wanting to.

⁊ᴓ

My child told me it wasn't what she wanted.
I don't want this, she said. *I don't want this.*
What does she know? I thought.
She doesn't know what she does and doesn't want,
she's just a child.
I wanted this to be true.

⁊ᴓ

Love God and do what you will,
said Augustine.
Some translations have want.
Want and will are similar, but not the same.

⁊ᴓ

They put veils over their wants
as they walked them through streets in bright sunlight.
It would be unseemly to have everyone stare.

஀

We wanted different things, said the Queen.
Meaning: I don't really know what he wanted
but whatever it was, I wasn't that interested.

஀

Name your wants
that they might socialise.

஀

She took the one I wanted! Sobbed my child.
I wanted that one!

I know, I said. *I know, it isn't fair.*
Together we sat down and wept.

஀

The King shrugged, saying: *Do what you want.*
Meaning: I love you.
I would do anything for you; I may die for you,
I haven't yet decided.

஀

And if they photographed want
held it to the light . . .

Still it would not be still.

෯෧

I wanted to kill it.
Here, I said. *Drink this.*

The want just smiled like a mother
and gently stroked my face.

The Night I Died

My heart had been shucked out like an oyster, yet I lived
on, long enough to write goodbyes to my children, my mother – halfway
through her letter I remembered she was dead herself.
                                        I touched the cavity where
my heart had been, white ceramic like a soap dish splashed with blood,
until amidst the mess of crossings out there came clarity, a moment of
commitment, as when you walk that tunnel to the belly
                              of an aeroplane, and I was leaving it behind,
my life.   You have to die, my dying self reminded me,
It's happening sooner than you thought, that's all.

What had I to show? Petty worries, yellow fields, friendships, wasted
hours in startled ordinary rain.

My heart was gone, not coming back, and yet I felt no dread, I moved
vertically
through something like dry ice, up into a vast and velvet black, nervous
but excited too – released –
                              and in this state I woke, heard a child call and went to
her, led her to the bathroom,
balanced her warm weight, held her while she peed.

Moths

poured in from back gardens
or abandoned dreams,   flotsam,
pieces of ourselves   returned
in air,
eyelids snipped from the dead
& made to fly,

        discarded elbow skins,
fingertips,   lips preserved and ironed flat,
nothing to say but

Brightness! Brightness!

Poured in from ages past,
pages of them sprung from reference books,
detailed in sharp 2B,
Fan-foot,   Clouded Silver,
Willow Beauty,

white or dull, or black
like this Old Lady in her widow's weeds.

Dainty Goths   tiny cloths
for cobweb bobbing

what obsession for this shade-less bulb.
What fuss!

Close the door, they settle, love the wall
so cool, so flushed
with light,
open it &
this emergency!   Suddenly too dead

then too alive.

Most make their way back to the dark,
their unexpected fat and feathery bodies crawling
scratchy-legged
on our tiles.   Not all escape.

This one floats on toilet water.
Lift it out and look at it, yellowed corner
of a love letter   it may yet live.

Snails

Now life is small and slow
we see them everywhere, even on the dustbin lid
in rainy dusk   shells
glistening like earrings.
That one lone adventurer
          suckered
to the centre of the kitchen window.

She hunts in verges, lifts and rattles empty cases
hoping for a body.
          If there's a shattered lump I kick it clear,
manoeuvre her away.
          Not fast enough today.   Snail!

She evades my hand,
          squats down to have her fill of this pitiable
weeping crush, stares a long time at its final
                    wondrous shame,
sits back on her haunches, unappalled.

Mercy

Whatever may ravage us tomorrow
has not come today,
and so my children are still young,
my body is their tree
and we have no safe distances.

Sleeve to sleeve I peg out shirts.
White sky, if you won't promise anything,
why should I complain?

The Field

What month would it have been when they pulled the turnips? She only told the story once, and was I properly listening?

I must have asked her questions, must have pictured that small incident then, as I picture it now, father and daughter stooped over turnip rows, bending their backs to the work. And it was work, dreary and tiring, but she'd been called and so she went. Why her? Because she wouldn't argue; timid, tall, common target of his rage, safest in a book and living someone else's life. He, who never had a warm word called, and so she went.

As I imagine it they labour silently. It's years ago this little incident, the telling of the little incident, lodged in darkness like a seed, and now at any moment mid-way through the washing up, or pushing swings, the seed coat ruptures and she nudges out, my mother with her girl's pale limbs unfurling, long adolescent legs, and lashing horizontally the Southland wind, for this is New Zealand's southern isle where the cold comes hard. Or is the season wrong? Is this instead ferocious sun? Is my young mother growing yet more freckled in the heat? No, in that imagined past it's neither blasting cold nor blazing heat. The sky is white. Beyond the field is also white, unwritten, nowhere to be, not school, or the basilica for mass, only this field.

In silence she pulls turnips then, whitish-purple, clotted with mud, row upon row until, how does it happen, how exactly does the letter drop from her cardigan pocket – or is it a coat – no matter, it falls to the ground, the letter falls. He notices and before she can fetch it up, he reaches down and lifts it clear of the earth. Her letter in his hands. The letter she has written to her cousin – which cousin, where? – and there they stand in the turnip field, Patrick O'Connell, six feet four, pale as the bleached sky and fierce as the sun. He puts his thumb to the envelope, property of his silent daughter whose melancholy rages him. She will not, can not argue him away from what he does, which is to read. And what does he read? Paddy O'Connell, strong as an ox, reads about himself from the pen of his wordless child. She writes of his travels to Ireland. She tells how she wishes he'd never come back.

The sounds of the earth continue, birds or the wind making small noises, and my grandfather, this man my mother used to pray would disappear, replaces her letter in its envelope and hands it back. Nothing is said. They return to the task. How old is she? Fourteen perhaps, let's say fourteen, the rest of her life blank space around the edges of the field. My grandfather's hands, the thumbnail ridged with dirt, and my mother not meeting his eye as she takes the letter, returns it to her pocket over and over and over again

Suburban Park Rosary

You say a rosary around the park,
mid-March, mid-morning, two weeks into Lent,
you pray not knowing how prayer leaves its mark.

Blessed art thou dog, thy clueless bark!
Blessed wind-blown daffodils, near spent!
You say each decade walking round the park.

You should be earning money, what a lark –
do fifty-three Hail Marys pay the rent?
You pray despite each rising question mark.

Your mother took her mysteries to the dark,
You kept her beads, half-knowing what they meant,
and now you walk them round and round the park

past silver birches peeling silver bark
and rusting swings which sound like a lament,
somehow these repetitions leave a mark:

what theologian understands the spark
that brings the Holy Spirit's warm descent?
You say a rosary around the park.
You pray not knowing how prayer leaves its mark.

Afternoon Sky

changing its white mind

combed with birds

resting

lover of all things equally

years and years old, years

and years

forgetting all of them

My Mother as Bernadette

then she sifted air,
brought her hands
                  to her face,
entranced,   moved them in slow circles,
as if washing.

        Was she practicing the old
rituals of life before they could be
dispensed with for good?
                        Was it that,

or was she like Bernadette,
commanded by Our Lady to dig
down into mud,

        a peasant girl
washing her face
in the slurry, scooping up
                the miraculous water.

Boxes

When sunlight decorates
the trees, and all the earth
is glad for life

I cut my mother's lawn.
The grass is ankle high,
the mower jams.

A robin ventures
down the washing line
to hear me curse;

I free the blades and fill
my hands with clumps
of staining green,

empty the collection box,
a wretched too-small
plastic thing.

Around a pool
of shaven grass
the robin pecks

for up-flung bugs,
considers me
with black-bright eyes,

my human grubbing
at the ground.
Is this my red-

scarfed mother, then?
Peculiar the fancies
we cook up.

Perhaps it saw her
at the window
scratching for a meal?

Or did she throw it crusts.
Who knows, she's flown.
Away! Away!

Little bird, when you
are dead who'll bury you?
You've just

your feathers, no one
shall pick apart
your nest or hanker

for your song.
But we must box
our days and sift

our Christmas cards,
wonder what
to give away

and what to keep
and how to live with it.
The grass is cut

and uncut too.
The boxes must be filled.
What work we do.

Lull

then into the nest
of my cupped hands

flies God – my bird –
ruffling into the heart

of my heart where
he settles and stays

for a while, singing.

Forgetting

I'll forget your four-year-old's voice,
forget its slightly comic husk, forget there was a night,
    tonight,   when you woke
crying your cheek hurt,   forget how I put my hand to feel heat.
Had you bitten it in your sleep? Was it your neck, cricked,
    tricking you with pain? Was it a dream?   But no
    you couldn't
shake it free,   hooked your arm around my neck
    and so I pressed my hands around your face
to find the ache,
        left you, fetched
a compress, Paracetamol,   chased your cries back upstairs
settled that new warmth beside your ear   waited
for your breaths to regulate,   grow deep,
watched you fall back into sleep,   one arm flung beside
your head, the way you'd slept newborn, those
other bedrooms   traceless now.

In Praise of Ailment

Why should the body be reduced to perfect health?
Most of us are only ever semi-well or glossing over it,

our ulcers undisclosed, all the gone wrong never quite put right,
bone ache, the pain of coughing up jewel-studded phlegm,

imperfect sleep with dreams that taste of vinegar. Surely the mind
is sickly nearly all the time, housed in its secret sanatorium.

Our maladies are necessary, they purify the uninfected hours
when we're forgotten by our bodies, sprawled thoughtless

in a swimming pool, airborne with lovemaking or simply
moving through October woods, tree to tree, limbs working

in an oiled gold, the back unlocked, the breath at last set free.

Statue of the Virgin in a Cuban-themed Restaurant

Was she salvaged
from a disused church,
or hauled from bric-a-brac?
Her little finger
is lost at the knuckle.
Some Creative had a vision
of her glorified amidst tequila
oozing gold, a basket
of fresh limes at her feet.

On Lower Marsh the offices
are turning out, the skies
of Waterloo grow velvety,
the evening alive
with what might be.
A plaster dancing girl
flings up her hand, mid-rumba.
Come in! She cries, *This is Havana!*
The Virgin too extends her arms,
Our Lady Queen of Sorrows,
Queen of Hope.

Yet Even Now

return, unwise and over-educated, unrepentant, penitent,
wear ashes if you must – don't lurk, ignore the silverfish – yet even now
    as ghosts
of you pass through each other in
and out of corridors, return –

return to me forgetting who you were,
uneven days, your high jumps higher than your praise –
return in winceyette, in camel hair, in lamé, rayon, silk,
return bedimmed in washing-powder whites,

bring second thoughts
bring songs to which you've misremembered tunes –

return in tracksuit pants you don't do running in – return
with matted hair or hair
you've made a hobby of – tipped pink, bouffed up –
return to me

your eyes electric blue – each lash electric too – return in nothing but
    those rags
you wear for bed – or wear your party gear – you love a party! –
parties where you dance and drink your fill
and empty on the journey home –

return on foot, on hobbyhorse, on stilts, on blasted wagons hitched to
sorrow-laden nags,
return on skiis you're ill equipped to use,
return on stolen bikes, in cars you've wrecked –

waving foreign flags, return,
whistling in cadet uniform, return,
return, your fingers lost, still drumming out a rhythm to their days,
return to me
I see you from the hill, pigswill freckling your shirt.

Return, your homework never to be done.
Return, your marriage never to be fixed.
Return, chewing your lips, your sleeve, kissing your teeth, return with
    words
dissolving in your throat, half-in half-out the window with your hoard.

Return to me beyond repair. Return to me, worm-infested, broke.
Return undetoxed – never mind the 12-step plan –
aflap with sticking plasters, fillings crumbling loose.

Return dressed up as someone else – I know your face.
Return despite the home you've modelled on your dream, and oh, despite
your influence, your affluence, your social ease, return.

Birds

City pigeons on their livid legs, or sometimes hobbling
on stumps like nightmare ballerinas.
Gulls, Jurassic and incensed, opening their beaks, opening
                                        and opening.
At the petting farm, half a dozen little girls
crowd around a heated box where chicks clump
underneath fluorescent light –
some have outgrown the space, they peck each other
flashing raw pink skin. The girls pass baby birds
from hand to hand like living pom-poms.

Here. One of the six-year-olds offers me a chick,
and I refuse. *Why?* It is a child's why,
a need to reach the nub. Because. Because I'm scared of it,
this fluff on twiggy bone? Because many years ago
a kibbutz hen house with its dense dark squawks and stench
made me want to run, the farm boys
chucking one another living, frightened birds.

The child waits, the chick inside her hands.
It won't hurt, she says.
And so I open up my hands, receive its yucky little legs
and frantic heart. The child watches us. *You see*, she tells me
with the satisfaction of a mother. *See?*

Flannery O'Connor

At five years old she owned a chicken that walked backwards
and made the Pathé News: there she is in black
and white, little Mary O'Connor
shouldering a scrabbling bird.

At twenty-five, with the lupus taking hold, she returns
to Georgia, fills the farm with birds:
chickens, naturally, also pheasants, quail, geese,
A tribe of mallard ducks, and finally, because she can resist
no longer, king of birds, the peacock.

In time the peacocks will surround her,
strutting like the proud fools of her fiction,
unswayable, utterly themselves.

They eat her mother's flowers.
They eat her uncle's figs.
They sit on fence posts, causing all of them to lean.
Her quest is at an end.
Truth, beauty; she distrusts pious phrases,
Particularly when they issue from my mouth.

But the peacocks have won her. Forty of them occupy the farm,
visitors gape at the slow rotation of their fanned tails.
One old woman cries Amen!

Forty peacocks, a wilful sort of craziness, and yet essential
as her daily Eucharist, which will draw her
to the last, the eye
of a peacock feather, perfect and astonishing.

Michelangelo's Late Drawings

Nearly blind, it's all behind him now.
Four scaffolded years risking a fall
like Adam's and the wrath of Julius
who struck him once for being slow.
Gone, the strength for travertine, all the figures
he could loosen have been freed,
and he's burned his studies, hundreds of them,
let them go, those young men twisting
in their mighty attitudes, bodies floating heavenwards
in specks of white. So much done, and yet he works
all night sometimes, light pooling
from the candle in his makeshift crown,
a stick of graphite as he fills what's left of time,
Love crucified, dying and living in the line.

November

When she could do no more than hang
between worlds,
or perhaps it was a slipping
out of time, as if stepping from a diving board
into suspending air,
I put my mouth beside
her ear and urged her free.

And when her little breath gave out
what came was such tranquillity
that I was homesick
for before my birth, and in that moment said aloud
You clever girl,
as if I were her midwife
and delivering her.

Song

Afterwards,
she held me

in the quiet hours,
led me from

that plot we laid her
under earth

no looking back
across an empty field,

no imagining
her un-becoming

what she was.
Her showings slid

like clouds inside
my new imagination:

it was hers, the place
where I began

to live, like that
abandoned home

she'd made
inside herself.

I lived there knowing
nothing of the days,

but floated thoughtless
as she fed me,

sang to me, and in
the early morning

whispered me awake,
her hand upon

the drum-skin
of my world;

her breath, her sighs.

Equinox

    with you slipped off, gone gently like a swept leaf,
I stand in the centre of my life
    or what might be the centre,
and feel it tilt.

All Souls

Who can fathom them
plucked out of time –
all their shopping bags set down for good?
How far are they
from reaching the sublime?

The Cantor sings *Lord God of Hosts*
and we depart.

A ruined pumpkin in the street,
its orange skull
caved in, but otherwise the paper ghosts
are cleared away, the terrace windows
lived in, bright.

At home I rustle up a bacon sandwich
for my own impromptu feast, a feast of salt
and fat.
            What happens now you both
no longer eat?

Imagination hits a wall.   Memory slips in –
the two of you manoeuvre round each other
in that kitchen
with the sunflower blind, still living lives
of lists and kids, listening
                  to a radio like this one play.

Snow

In these startling deep drifts

I think of them

a hundred miles away

beneath fresh quilts of snow,

together / not together,

body beside body, like us,

not touching as we sleep.

Afterlife

my life was shown to me at super speed
flickering faster than the Skybox forwarding ×30
and there I was in jogging pants and
slipper boots curled in a wine-coloured
armchair watching something dismal on TV –
a show where cameras follow strangers flung
together in some pre-determined circumstance,
strangers forced to make the best of it, although
of course already they can't stand each other,

and while they gather seeds for arguments,
the great clock of my life is counting down
and a crowd of angels dance around the set
doing their seraphic best to heave me up,
to haul me out of it – away! Away! –
                              but I can't see them yet.

Sunflowers, September

Too often now
they're shivery,
tattered, catching at us
with their ruined looks.
Which of us
could drag them
by the roots, even
this one with its head
half gone.
Don't their centres
still sleep bees,
or one at least,
we've seen it curled
and dozing
in a deep brown sun.

Ungainly girls,
they've held us too
this shrunken summer,
graced our little
lives, reminders
of what yellow
means, looming gladly
every time we pass –
did they really
spring from nothing
but a chip of
button, ridge of toenail
clipping, joke
of seed?

We've learned
to wait. We'll wait
until they reach
their last, each floret
dropped, each
leaf a failure.
Even as they bend
towards the earth
their heads are packed
with other lives. *Next year*,
they say. *Next year*.

Unequal Love

'For a wonderful physical tie binds the parents to the children; and – by some sad, strange irony – it does not bind us children to our parents.' – E. M. FORSTER

So I watch you from the window
crossing shadow into sun,

the grass is high, you wade in deep,
as if your eyes were on someone;

say you'll never turn forever,
never hurt your fond old thing,

never find it's me who's calling,
lift the phone and let it ring.

You will of course, I had a mother,
she was frail with love like me,

she stood at a kitchen window,
thought these thoughts, saw what I see.

Windows, gardens, children, mothers,
time can offer no reprieve,

love's unequal, love's forgotten,
kiss their faces, let them leave.

On a Theme by Augustine

'Animals, and even lifeless things, praise you through the lips
of those who contemplate them.' (*The Confessions* 5.2)

In my nonsense let me make a blessing of this stone, this chinked
and broken flint, two inches in diameter, white vein flowing
through its smooth school-jumper-coloured heart; this relic of
your dream, discreet and trodden on, who if it could would surely
thank you for its necessary work, its job of doing nothing much
but sitting in this fallow flower bed five steps from the garage door.
How perfectly anonymous its rind of garden dirt, no stony little
fingers drumming at the ground, no hat to tip, no sound, no sound.

Does it praise you? No, it lies inert, cloistered as a Carmelite, and
waits for spring, or rather doesn't wait because it has no mind to
know its seasons. Does it praise you? No

– and yet it does, but only if you let me say it does, and so I write
this down and do.

Scenes from Life on Earth

I loved the trees,
I didn't learn their names
but muddled them
into one gorgeous lanky family;

I loved their cool, slim hips
their sudden splits
their tender dark
their never ending want for sky;

I loved their interlaced attentiveness
their flair for being still
or keeping time with any
off-beat breeze.

I loved the trees because
they had redemption down,
oh God be glorified, I loved the trees!
The way they ate their old regrets
                      and made them into leaves.

Acknowledgements

Thanks to the editors of the following journals, in which some of these poems first appeared: *America Magazine, Amethyst Review, Bad Lilies, Magma, The New Statesman, The North, Poetry London, Poetry Ireland Review, The Poetry Review, Wild Court*

'Tomato Plant Survival Song' was shortlisted for the Montreal International Poetry Prize 2020 and published in the anthology.

Thanks to dear friends who have helped during the writing of this book, particularly all the members, past and present, of the Norwich poetry group. Thanks also to Judy Brown, Kathryn Maris, Sarah Ridgard, Deborah Arnander, Clare Jarrett, Lynne Bryant, Sarah Law and Sally Read. Special thanks to Lisa Smith for her enduring friendship. My love to Stephen, Esther and Clara.

Thank you to Chris Hamilton-Emery for making a home for this collection, and my gratitude to Cornelia Parker for kindly allowing the use of her artwork on the cover.

Notes

'Flannery O'Connor'
Quotes taken from the essay, 'Living with a Peacock' by Flannery O'Connor and a letter from Flannery to Betty Hesler, 1955 (Published in *The Habit of Being*).

'My Mother as Bernadette'
Bernadette Soubirous (1844–1879), later Saint Bernadette of Lourdes.

'Spencer in the Wilderness'
In 1938–39 Stanley Spencer lived alone for six months in Swiss Cottage after losing his home to his second wife, Patricia Preece. There he began an unfinished series of paintings, *Christ in the Wilderness*.

This book has been typeset by
SALT PUBLISHING LIMITED
using Sabon, a font designed by Jan Tschichold
for the D. Stempel AG, Linotype and Monotype Foundries.
It is manufactured using Holmen Book Cream 65gsm,
a Forest Stewardship Council™ certified paper from the
Hallsta Paper Mill in Sweden. It was printed and bound
by Clays Limited in Bungay, Suffolk, Great Britain.

CROMER
GREAT BRITAIN
MMXXII